I0879856

Flipping the Classroom

Flipping the Classroom

What Every ESL Teacher Needs to Know

Robyn Brinks Lockwood
Stanford University

University of Michigan Press
Ann Arbor

First paperback edition 2023

Published in the United States of America by the
University of Michigan Press

Paperback ISBN: 978-0-472-03954-8
Ebook ISBN: 978-0-472-12453-4

First published March 2018

ACKNOWLEDGMENTS

I would like to thank my editor, Kelly Sippell, for her valuable input during the development of this e-book and her dedication to producing materials that can help instructors be even better at what they do in the classroom. Many thanks to all the students who have taken my classes at Stanford University and who worked diligently and with great participation in my classes. They didn't even know they were participating in flipped lessons or a flipped classroom, but it was their progress and development that made me realize that flipping was not just good for me, but also good for them. Thanks, as always, to my parents, both former teachers, for their encouragement to do what is best for the students; and my husband, a former engineering professor, whose stories about his own students' needs in mainstream classes helped me better structure my own ESL classroom. And, to my favorite boys: Tim, Darrin, and Nathan—I'm so proud of you all.

To all the teachers who want to try flipping, please do. It has made a world of difference for students and for my teaching. Good luck! Let me know how it goes.

CONTENTS

Introduction

Why Did I Flip?

I come to campus early every morning. I find the early mornings on campus quiet and peaceful, and I've learned that I can read many student research papers and prepare for my classes before everyone else wakes up. But before that, I stop for coffee at the campus bookstore and pick up a copy of the campus newspaper, *The Stanford Daily*. It was the January 10, 2013 edition of the paper that changed my teaching from what I had been doing for most of my career to what I'd happily been doing for the past four years. It also led me to write my book, *Flip It! Strategies for the ESL Classroom*.*

The front page of the paper ran an article titled "Flipped classroom gaining popularity among profs." Because I had classes to prepare for, I had intended to just skim the paper. However, the article caught my attention at first because I recognized colleagues' names from the departments—primarily in the STEM fields—that my students tend to study in. These professors had flipped their classrooms and were very pleased with the results. The article shared that the flipped classroom model was growing in popularity and that not only did instructors like it, students liked it too. Instructors felt rejuvenated and students seemed to appreciate this "new" way of teaching. Grant applications, which many of us in the field of ESL have a love–hate relationship with, were being submitted by all these other departments for flipped classroom support. Nearly half of those received partial or full funding.

I did set aside the paper that morning. After all, it was the beginning of winter term and I had classes that day. However, I could not put the idea out of my mind. A quick online search led me to discover that flipped classrooms extended well beyond my own university. They existed across the country in a variety of disciplines and at a variety of levels. Since this wasn't something simply being adopted by one professor at one university, I knew I needed to pay attention.

---

* *Flip It! Strategies for the ESL Classroom* can be found at press.umich.edu.

The term **flipped** is commonly paired with several words: **flipped learning**, **flipped classrooms**, or **flipped instruction**, to name a few. It also had several aliases, such as **reverse instruction**, **inverted classrooms**, **reverse teaching**, or **backwards teaching**. It also wasn't that "new—just new to me to language learning. Soon I realized that this was not going to be a passing fad or a catchphrase we would hear about for a while before it faded away, only to be replaced with another fad or catchphrase. Regardless of when, where, or how you flip, and no matter which term or alias you choose, it seemed that this approach was here to stay and that the benefits were outweighing the drawbacks.

More important, I realized the implications this was going to have on second language (L2) students and instructors. A main objective of my job is to prepare students to succeed academically with their coursework. If students were going to need to succeed in a flipped classroom, then I was not only going to have to teach them English—the other obvious main objective of my job—but I was also going to have to prepare them to succeed in a flipped classroom setting. I thought the best way to do this might be to flip my own classroom—or at the very least, flip some of my lessons. Plus, I selfishly wanted to experience the benefits that "flippers" were raving about—namely, feeling revitalized about teaching, more attentive students, providing a more student-centered classroom, etc. Why shouldn't I reap those same rewards and do the same thing for my students? After all, it is my job to serve my students.

In the end though, I decided this was worth a try because I was committed to making the classroom experience the best it could be for my students and for me.

How Do I Flip—and How Do I Flip the L2 Classroom?

Once the decision to flip my classroom was made, I pulled out the course outlines for my courses and began to figure out how to flip. I realized very quickly that I needed to learn more about flipping in general and to then figure out what I needed to do to flip a second language classroom. I started by thinking about what I knew about the concept.

If you conduct an online search of "flipped learning" or "flipped classrooms," you will find it described as an instructional strategy in which the teaching is provided online outside the classroom and homework is done inside the classroom. In short, what you usually find are three "steps":

1. Instructors videotape their lectures.
2. Students watch the lectures as homework.
3. Instructors and students participate together in class on projects, in discussions, or on "what used to be homework" about the videotaped lecture in the classroom.

At this point, I hesitated. I was not sure this "definition" of flipping would work in an L2 setting. First, I had some good textbooks that I wanted to keep using. They included what I needed to teach. They saved me time. I could not forget that I still taught ESL. The textbooks were pedagogically sound as well. They taught the skills students needed to apply to their other classes and to their language development.

Second, I was very concerned about the technology. Not only was I worried about learning to master whatever it was I would need to master to make the videos, I just didn't want to be on video. Some people are very photogenic, but I'm afraid that gene skipped right over me. More important though, I was more concerned about what to record. I didn't lecture formally the way instructors in other fields do. In scanning my course outlines, the closest things I had to lectures were the ones that accompanied my listening textbooks. Was I supposed to record myself talking about the strategies that were already presented so well in the textbooks? That didn't seem to make much sense to me. I began to think that flipping an L2 class might need to be different from the way other fields might flip.

Every discipline has unique features. For example, many science disciplines require experiments in a lab; others require or encourage internships. ESL is no different. Our needs and our students' needs don't necessarily fall neatly into a mold or particular method. So why couldn't flipping ESL be different? We always adjust our lessons and content based on the level of our students, our populations, and our content. Why couldn't we adjust our flipped classroom as well?

At a conference later in 2013, I talked with my editor about flipping in ESL. There might be other ESL teachers like me who wanted to flip but weren't sure how it would work. The idea of an ESL teacher's resource on flipping seemed of interest. I thought it might be worth exploring the idea of a teacher's resource for ESL teachers with a few ideas and some sources for teachers who wanted to start flipping. Hence, *Flip It! Strategies for the ESL Classroom* was born.

Flip It! is a resource that methodically guides teachers as they take steps to begin flipping their ESL classrooms. It documents some of the quick and easy ways I started flipping, without making videos orgiving up my textbooks, to begin flipping a classroom. The book includes more than fifty activities from ESL textbooks to illustrate the types of activities that can be flipped and spans the various skills: reading, writing, listening, speaking, grammar, and vocabulary.

The development of that book came after I flipped all my ESL classes. Some are more flipped than others. In other words, I sometimes flip lessons or flip half the class rather than every single session. Since 2013, I have flipped and have never looked back. I've learned to implement the flipped learning model with all the skills.

As I looked back at my academic career—as a student and as a teacher—I realized that the way we learn and the way we teach has changed considerably. When I was a student, I wasn't in a flipped classroom. I sat for 50 or 75 minutes and took notes during a lecture. Then I would study those notes and do whatever homework was assigned. There were many classes in which I never interacted with my classmates, and I certainly never interacted with the instructor beyond an occasional meeting during office hours. I am lucky to be the daughter of two fabulous teachers who always inspired me to want to learn, but I do wonder about today's students, who may not have had the same support system I was fortunate enough to have. Could a flipped or partially flipped classroom actually provide more support for students, since the instructor is working with the students more in the classroom?

Continuing to develop my own flipped classroom has caused me to reflect on the questions I had (and some of the prevailing myths) when I first started my journey to flipping my classroom. Those reflections have led to this e-book, and I hope that by sharing these questions and answers that worked for me, other teachers might be able make the decision to flip their second language classrooms. For those who are interested in more information about how flipped classrooms benefit students and teachers, sample activities suited to flipping from ESL textbooks, and other specific tips and strategies for flipping the classroom, see *Flip It! Strategies for the ESL Classroom* (https://www.press.umich.edu/7110704/flip_it!).

1. What Is Flipping?

You've decided you either want to or need to flip your classroom. If you're like me, then that means you want to know more about flipped learning as a concept to make sure you do it right and in the best way for your students, setting, and content. I quickly learned that there is more than one way to flip, and I also discovered that flipping did not mean that not every single moment of every single class needed to be flipped.

Other Modes and Models

When I first started flipping, I attended the Teaching Professor Technology Conference and became aware of other related models and terminology—MOOCs (Massive Open Online Courses), online courses, blended learning, mixed-mode learning, hybrid learning, and so on. What were these models and should I be considering them instead of flipping?

MOOCs have grown quite popular. A MOOC is a course delivered completely online. Anyone can enroll in a MOOC; no one is denied, and there is no cap on enrollment (that's why the M stands for "massive"). When MOOCs first started, both the course materials and the content were free to students. Since then, more large universities have offered MOOCs. The course materials are more likely to be licensed now, but attendance is still usually free. Regardless, a MOOC was not an option for me. My department caps our enrollment and languages are taught in-person in the classroom.

Online courses are also becoming more and more popular in today's digital world. These courses deliver the content completely online, and students can use any device to access the information. They also have the freedom to access it anytime from anywhere. Many of these courses are instructor-led. It is likely that the instructor and students are not online at the same time, but there is student-teacher interaction. Additionally, these courses could have restricted enrollment, could be graded or credit-bearing, and could have certain requirements in terms of homework, participation, and assignments. Many online courses have fees associated with them, although prices vary widely. Some online programs that are popular are Coursera, edX, Udemy, Udacity, Codecademy, Bloc, iversity, Skillshare, and General Assembly.

I also became familiar with the term **synchronous** in relation to online courses. These courses are completely online as well, but they do require teachers and students to be online at the same time for discussions. These, too, are not "massive" and have limited enrollment.

Whether synchronous or not, online courses weren't an option for me. My classes are face-to-face classes at a "bricks and mortar" university. But what about blended, mixed-mode, or hybrid courses? I wanted to make sure flipped learning was indeed the best option for me.

Blended learning is a combination of traditional classroom or face-to-face learning with online learning. It is not a distance education course or a solely online course because there is some face-to-face time and only part of the classroom time is replaced by an online component. **Mixed-mode learning** or **hybrid learning** are aliases for blended learning. This learning model can be a good alternative for institutions with student populations that cannot attend classes full-time because classroom time can be significantly less than what is traditional. The model does not reduce the amount of content, nor does it completely remove the face-to-face component. Students are required to attend classes at scheduled times and places. With blended learning, a website or course management system of some sort is required. A certain level of technical savvy and access to digital devices is required for both instructors and students.

Some people may classify flipped learning as a type of blended, mixed-mode, or hybrid learning since there is a video component along with class time, yet it is different because there is not as much class time. In contrast, in a flipped learning classroom, there is exactly the same amount of classroom time/contact hours as there always was.

Time factors were an important consideration for me and for all teachers. My university teaches in-person classes that meet twice weekly for 80 minutes each. I wasn't allowed, nor did I want, to cut my face-to-face time, and I certainly wasn't going to be able to cut it in half. That meant that some of these other models would not work for me.

Also, I wasn't willing to sacrifice my textbooks. In the cases where other instructors teach the same class, we all had to use the same book. We don't necessarily teach the same way, but it is a book that the entire department uses. If I was going to flip, I had to keep using the textbook and cover the same amount of material as my colleagues.

Then there's technology. I was not prepared to be reliant on technology. One of the benefits to a flipped classroom (over other models) is that the content is always available to students. Despite the pervasiveness of technology and living in Silicon Valley, wireless access or technology access might not always be available. Even a power outage can affect access to online material! Also, I work in a setting where technology is readily available on a university campus, so technological proficiency was not a problem for my college students. But I wondered about settings such as the one I volunteer in (an adult education program); some adult education programs have computer labs, but not all of them have the technological resources. Even if a school has these kinds of resources, some students might not have them at home, so access to technology is an important factor to consider before flipping. Lack of or limited technology doesn't prevent flipping, but it does impact how material is presented to students and their access must be considered.

Therefore, because of its flexibility with content delivery and the amount of face-to-face time, flipped learning was the best option for me. Knowing that I would be required to have the same amount of class meetings, I refocused my attention on flipped classrooms, but I did alter my approach. I needed to stop thinking of it as a classroom model and view it as *a learning model*. I didn't necessarily want to flip my classroom, but I did want to flip the learning. So, flipped learning became my goal. I soon discovered that some flipping required only small changes to instruction and lesson plans, while other ideas and certain classes required more thought. Starting slowly and adapting as I needed to for students and content allowed me to flip efficiently and effectively.

Basic Tenets of Flipped Learning

The Flipped Learning Network (2014)† developed this definition for flipped learning:

> Flipped learning is a pedagogical approach in which direct instruction moves from the group learning space to the individual learning space, and the resulting group space is transformed into a dynamic, interactive learning environment where the educator guides students as they apply concepts and engage creatively in the subject matter.
>
> (Source: https://flippedlearning.org/definition-of-flipped-learning/)

† For more information, find the Flipped Learning Network at https://flippedlearning.org

The Flipped Learning Network (2014) also provides the four pillars of flipped learning:

F = Flexible Environment
L = Learning Culture
I = Intentional Content
P = Professional Educator

It's fairly easy to see why many people believe that homework becoming classwork is one of the basic tenets of a flipped classroom. It is true that flipped learning is different than the traditional classroom in which an instructor stands in front of the class and presents the content students need to know. The phrase "sage on the stage" describes this more traditional model, but flipped learning occurs when students are exposed to the instruction outside the classroom and when class time is used for what used to be homework—application of newly learned knowledge.

Most of what my colleagues who were flipping were doing matched what I had heard so much about—they recorded their lectures and then students watched those on their own. Then, what used to be homework becomes classwork. The classwork would then be more interactive:class activities might be discussion or debates, group projects, or presentations. It really depends on the class. For example, in STEM classes, students might work on the problem sets or equations in class, conduct experiments, or discuss results. The difference being that when the "old" homework is done in class, the instructor transitions from being "sage on the stage" to "guide on the side" and is there to assist and talk with students while they do what used to be homework.

However, it's more than just that. Flipped learning is not simply video lectures and then swapping homework for classwork and classwork for homework. It is more than the F or Flexible Environment (students learning when and where they want via the videos) and L for Learning Culture (a more interactive classroom with the teacher serving as a guide on the side). The I (or Intentional Content) is important: Teachers need to be intentional with their planning, making sure that the content moved out of the classroom is at a level students can comprehend on their own—that it's accessible and relevant to the students. It is also true that classroom activities are student-centered whenever possible.

The Influence of Bloom's Taxonomy

A key element of flipping learning involves Bloom's taxonomy (a **taxonomy** is a classification of something—here, educational learning objectives in terms of complexity and specificity). Flipped learning turns Bloom's taxonomy upside down. Rather than class time focusing on the two lowest levels of Bloom's skills, students do this "easier" work on their own. Class time is then spent on the four higher-level skills in Bloom's taxonomy that are often much harder for students to do on their own or not practiced at all. Readers can view a version of the traditional taxonomy in *Flip It!* or via an internet search.

The original Bloom's taxonomy was published in 1956 and included six developmental categories focused on the three major domains of learning: cognitive, affective, and psychomotor. The six categories in the order they originally appeared were:

- Evaluation
- Synthesis
- Analysis
- Application
- Comprehension
- Knowledge

The two lowest levels focused solely on acquisition of knowledge. As students move up through the categories, they demonstrate what they have learned until finally they reach the higher levels where they are able to demonstrate that they can use the knowledge to create their own ideas or projects.

The two lowest levels of Bloom's taxonomy, Knowledge and Comprehension, are taught in a traditional classroom setting: The "sage on the stage" presents the material, and students demonstrate their understanding with a variety of exercises, practices, or activities. Then, they are sent home with an assignment that requires them to use higher-level skills. Essentially, students are asked to complete the "harder" activities on their own. Or, perhaps worse—they are assigned additional comprehension-level activities and are never asked to work on the higher levels of the taxonomy.

In a flipped classroom, the taxonomy itself is flipped: The students work on the two "easiest" and the lower-level skills on their own, and activities using the higher-level skills are done in the classroom where the "guide on the side" or Professional Educator (the P in FLIP) is there to assist.

In the 1990s, Bloom's taxonomy was revised by one of Bloom's students. The levels were changed from nouns to verbs, Evaluation was moved down a level, and it was replaced with Creating. So, the new levels (again, in the order they originally appear) are:

- Creating
- Evaluating

- Analyzing
- Applying
- Understanding
- Remembering

It doesn't matter which taxonomy is used, the general concept is the same: The two lower levels of the taxonomy are moved out of the classroom, while the four higher levels of the taxonomy are moved into the classroom. When you flip the revised taxonomy, the levels are in this order:

- Remembering
- Understanding
- Applying
- Analyzing
- Evaluating
- Creating

The Understanding and Remembering levels are "homework" and the other skills or levels—Applying, Analyzing, Evaluating, and Creating—are done in the classroom with the guide on the side or the professional educator. Moving forward, only the revised Bloom labels will be used.

The taxonomy can be used regardless of student level (beginning, intermediate, advanced), setting (elementary, secondary, or university), or content (an ESL skill such as reading, writing, listening, speaking, vocabulary, or grammar). What is most important is to be intentional about the content being moved in and out of the classroom. This also makes the P or Professional Educator in flipped learning important in two ways: (1) identifying the best content to move in and out of the classroom and (2) deciding how to serve as a guide on the side.

In summary, there are two basic tenets to remember about flipped classrooms. The first is relatively easy and straightforward: Material traditionally presented or done in class is assigned as homework, and tasks usually assigned as homework are moved into the classroom. The second is more challenging: Instructors need to make sure they are moving the right material out of or into the classroom. In other words, moving activities into the classroom won't be beneficial to students if it is an activity that simply is at the Remembering and Understanding levels on the new taxonomy and does not move students up on the taxonomy. *Teachers need to flip Bloom's taxonomy.* Activities that are assigned to be done out of the classroom need to be the low-level skills that students can do on their own; activities that are done inside the classroom need to use higher-level skills—at the Applying level or higher.

When I reflected on my own journey as a "flipper," I realized that I had not always done this. Grammar homework, for example, was often more exercises that never took students to higher levels on the taxonomy. If I sent students home with a verb tense activity that asked them to choose the correct verb tense, then they were doing nothing more than proving they had comprehended the basic information; they were not required to actually apply the verb tenses to other situations, which likely meant they would not know how to use it in the real world.

Additionally, flipped classrooms are known to be interactive and collaborative. However, just because a class is interactive, doesn't mean it is flipped. Again, if students are simply reading role-plays in a speaking class, the class may be talking and working together, but the work doesn't extend beyond the lower levels of the taxonomy—and that means it's not flipped.

Once I was able to adhere to those two basic tenets—swapping homework and classwork and literally flipping Bloom's taxonomy—I was able to dispel some of the myths about flipped learning myself and answer some of the biggest questions I had about this classroom model.

2. What About My Textbooks? (Myth: Flipped classes can't use textbooks.)

Anyone who has visited an academic conference and walked through the exhibit hall knows there are many publishers and content providers. Conducting a quick online search yields scores of ESL textbooks from which to choose for classroom adoption. I spent time and effort choosing textbooks that worked well for my classes because they taught the information, content, and skills that my students needed. This content also aligned with my course objectives and goals, which is why I had adopted the textbooks to begin with. Also—a key element that would become important when deciding to flip—the textbooks I use are accessible enough that students can gain the basic understanding of the material on their own. As mentioned too, I also used a textbook that was used across the department by several other instructors.

The bottom line: I liked my textbooks and did not want to give them up. Since my textbooks included the content I needed, I was determined to dispel the myth that flipping my classroom would require me to abandon the textbooks. In fact, flipping my class might actually allow students to use their textbooks *more*. A flipped classroom requires me to flip Bloom's taxonomy, meaning students learn content on their own—the Remembering and Understanding levels that are done outside of class. This information is *in the textbooks*. The textbook is written in an accessible way—it provides the content for students. The important point here is that the provision of the main content that students will need to perform higher-level tasks in class should be in a form that's accessible, and that might be in the textbook. The important consideration for teachers is to carefully choose which materials students study outside of class and which activities they complete on their own.

In most cases, deciding what students learn—the content presenting ideas or knowledge—is fairly straightforward. For example, in a grammar class, I would have normally presented whatever lesson was presented in a language box in the textbook. If time allowed, we would practice with some of the activities that follow the grammar presentation in the textbook. These activities might be multiple choice or fill in the blank, requiring students to identify or use the correct tense of the verbs. The activities helped me determine whether students understood the content. Then I would send students home to complete the more challenging activities—those that required higher-level skills—on their own. For example, if I were teaching verb tenses, I might ask students to read sentences where different tenses of the verbs are used and analyze how the tense changes the meaning. Or maybe I'd ask them to write a paragraph using the verb tense. In retrospect, these activities are more challenging and, although students often do understand the content (or claim to) before they leave the classroom, when they actually have to apply it to their own new work or other activities on their own, they struggle. The flipped classroom moves these harder-level skills into the classroom where the instructor is available to assist.

Additionally, if the Remembering and Understanding is happening at home, then sometimes I have additional class time to do more Applying. Let's continue with the example of verb tense lessons: I might plan a debate or discussion about current events if I wanted students to use present tense or I might create a role-play activity in which students participate in a courtroom, with each student playing a role such as witness, attorney, judge, or accused criminal. As students play out the court case, verb tenses are practiced. A wrong verb tense can change the "verdict." The court case can be recorded and students can analyze it later and note how the wrong verb tense might change the meaning of their testimony.

When flipping, it's important for teachers to pay close attention to the types of activities assigned as homework, bearing in mind that the homework should fall into the two lowest levels of Bloom's taxonomy. Read the direction lines in textbooks and notice the verbs used with the activity, or what action exactly is being required of the student. Verbs and actions associated with knowledge and comprehension are the activities that now need to be homework. In many cases, these were the activities that were assigned as homework in the traditional classroom.

List of Verbs Associated With Remembering (Now Done Outside the Classroom)

define
find
identify
label
list
locate

match
memorize
name
order
recall
recognize
repeat
reproduce
state
tell

List of Verbs Associated With Understanding (Now Done Outside the Classroom)

arrange
clarify
classify
demonstrate
describe
explain
identify
locate
outline
report
rephrase/restate
review
select
show
summarize
translate

Another reason I wanted to keep my textbooks is related to a basic tenet of flipped learning—the content is always available. Consider a traditional lecture setting. Once students hear a lecture, that spoken word disappears. Students have only their notes on which to rely. But in a flipped setting, the general content is always available. Having all the knowledge in a textbook is arguably always available to students outside of class, perhaps even more so than videos or online material, especially when students do not have access to technology.

Lesson Learned

Textbooks or printed materials are just as good as videos in the flipped learning environment. Whether it be printed or video content, when it comes to the basics of learning—Remembering and Understanding—what is important is that students can take as long as they want or need to learn the content and that the content is always available for students to review at any time they want. This is not always the case in a traditional classroom, where students work at different paces.

3. What About Technology? (Myth: Flipping requires videos and technological expertise.)

The second question that I faced and feared was about technology—would I have to make videos? I was happily able to dispel the myth that I needed to record my lectures on video if I wanted to flip my classroom, but I also learned more about the use of technology overall.

Using Videos In General

Without losing sight of the basic tenets—flipping classwork/homework and flipping Bloom's taxonomy—using videos is certainly a viable option. I wanted to begin flipping sooner rather than later, so part of my decision to avoid videos in the beginning was simply a matter of time. I was not sure I had the technological know-how to learn how to make videos, let alone how to make them quickly.

I also didn't have ready-made lectures (like professors in some disciplines). What exactly would I record? On days that ESL instructors "lecture" or present new content, we don't normally take the entire 50 or 75 minutes of class to deliver the content while students sit and take notes. What would we record?

What I discovered was that, although professors/instructors in the math, science, engineering, social sciences, and humanities fields do often give long lectures, a flipped classroom does not require long lectures on video. In fact, many people who flip use shorter videos; often, longer lectures are divided into smaller chunks and used that way.

Interestingly, the rise of the term **micro-lecture** is sometimes associated with online, blended, or flipped learning. One common alias is **mini-lecture**. These lectures are, by design, brief and woven into other activities that teach the content. The general consensus is that shorter pieces are better for student focus and comprehension.

Micro-lectures are also not one-dimensional; sometimes they include the instructor's face, sometimes they include PowerPoint slides with audio, or sometimes both. In a flipped setting, micro-lectures most often introduce the content, give examples, and/or explain and clarify concepts.

Any video that you create or use does not need to be "fancy" or professional-grade. In fact, it may not be visual at all; it could just be audio. Perhaps one of the most popular sites for micro-lectures is that of Khan Academy. Khan focuses primarily on traditional academic content, and it is free to use, making it a great choice for ESL teachers preparing students for academic content. Khan Academy is not-for-profit, so all videos are free and most not even 10 minutes in length. Another good option is Lynda.com, but it requires a subscription. The fee is reasonable and does provide unlimited access to more than 80,000 videos on a variety of topics. See https://www.khanacademy.org/ and https://www.lynda.com/ for videos to use in a flipped classroom.

Lecture content can be combined with other content, such as material in the course textbook, PowerPoint slides (in the video, posted online, or printed), photos/images, or other audio. For example, in a writing course, students may watch a video about paraphrasing and read the strategy box in the writing textbook about paraphrasing as the homework assignment. They may also complete a comprehension-level paraphrasing practice in the book. The video itself can be created by sending students to a variety of online sources such as YouTube channels, education websites, or school and university resources.

One of the myths I was most motivated to dispel was that the instructor had to be the one delivering the content via video. I did not want to "star" in my own videos. While there may be some advantages to that, it is certainly not a requirement. One easy way to start flipping is to start with a listening course. Many of the ESL textbooks are accompanied in some way with an audio or video component, which means that the technology component is already created. All the instructor needs to do is make sure that one of these options is possible: (1) Students buy the CD or DVD that accompanies the textbook; (2) the audio/video is available for upload to the course management system used at your school or for your course (or there is some other way for students to access the clips through the library or computer lab), or (3) the clips are available online. It is worth noting that audio only, or audio with PPT (PowerPoint presentation), or other visuals are options as well.

In a flipped classroom, students listen to or watch the materials outside of class. By doing this, the instructor adheres to the tenets of flipped learning: Students have access to the content anytime they want and they can listen or watch as many times (or as few times) as they need or want and the basic comprehension/understanding of the content is done outside of the class. Before flipping, much of my listening class was spent simply listening to the content and then the remaining time spent on comprehension-level activities—those well-known main idea and detail exercises. In many ways, this did a disservice to the students who eventually need to enter mainstream classes and professional careers that require them to not just understand but *use* the content.

One of the questions I am often asked about flipping is how I make sure students do the homework. One way to do this is to make the in-class activities high-stakes: Give a quiz in class or play a game that requires the content of the homework to be able to participate. Make sure that most of the class time is spent on Applying, Analyzing, Evaluating, and Creating activities.

Curation of Content

Teachers may be surprised how many videos already exist that can be used for ESL purposes. A key to success here has to do with curation. Instructors need to watch the videos to make sure the content is relevant to the course, textbook(s), and/or goals and that the level and length is appropriate. With flipped learning becoming more and more prevalent, it's not surprising that several YouTube channels have sprung up with the same people delivering content, so if consistency is important, these are a nice option. Ohio State University, for example, has videos available on its channel for academic writing, grammar, and idioms. JenniferESL has more than a half-million subscribers to her channel and adds new videos often.

A few examples of video series that can work for different classes are listed here (note: links change often):

Lectures for EAP (English for Academic Purpose) Preparation and Listening/Speaking Courses

- Academic Earth: http://academicearth.org
- Free Video Lectures: http://freevideolectures.com/
- Harvard Open Courses: Open Learning Initiative: http://www.extension.harvard.edu/open-learning-initative
- Open Yale Courses: http://oyc.yale.edu
- Stanford University's Frederick H. Hillier Series (designed for incoming international students): https://sites.stanford.edu/EFSLectures/
- MIT Open Courseware: https://ocw.mit.edu/courses/

Or, to make things simpler, use an indexing service of sorts to search for available lectures by topic. LectureFox is one such service: http://www.onlinecourses.com/lectures/. See also the Open Education Consortium website at http://www.oeconsortium.org/about-oec/.

Many professional, news, and educational websites also offer videos that can be used in class. Sometimes, these sites also offer transcripts that are useful when planning lessons and activities for class. Others provide handouts and lessons to accompany the video, making flipping the classroom even easier. To illustrate this point, StoryCorps offers a Thanksgiving lesson that practices speaking and listening, as well as research and critical-thinking skills. The teacher packet includes lesson plans, common core correlations, and worksheets (https://storycorpsme.s3.amazonaws.com/uploads/2016/11/StoryCorps-TGTL-Teacher-Toolkit-1.pdf). Also, government sites, whose topics are often covered in ESL textbooks, provide lesson plans and curriculum ideas. For example, many ESL textbooks have units on food and nutrition. The U.S. Department of Agriculture (USDA) offers several lesson plans. Once students practice the skills in the ESL textbook, they can then employ higher-level skills and use the content from the ESL reading or listening passage on the provided activities on the USDA website. A booklet is available at https://supertracker.usda.gov/Documents/SuperTracker%20Nutrition%20Lesson%20Plans%20for%20High%20School%20Students.pdf.

Some Other Sites Worth Exploring Include:

Discovery Education: http://www.discoveryeducation.com/
EdSitement (humanities): https://edsitement.neh.gov/lesson-plans
PBS: http://www.pbs.org/education/teacherslounge
NOAA: http://www.noaa.gov/education/for-educators
Smithsonian: http://www.smithsonianeducation.org/educators/index.html

Flipping is ideal to make sure students actually use the skills we are teaching them, whether that be skimming (as taught as a skill in reading class), recognizing speaker bias (as taught in listening class), persuading listeners (as taught in a speaking class), or summarizing (as taught in a writing class). Similarly, in grammar classes and vocabulary classes, we want students to apply the ideas, to extend their skill levels beyond memorizing information. Revisiting the grammar activity in which students stage and participate in a court case, a flipped grammar lesson might ask students to watch any video or read applicable sections of the textbook to learn, for example, *if/then* statements. Witness statements of the "crime" would require students on the jury to use the grammar (*If the witness saw . . . , then the accused thief could not have stolen . . .*). The same is true of vocabulary. If legal words are the lesson, then a court case or debate as to someone's guilt or innocence often requires students to use the words in context.

Making Your Own Videos

If you decide that you do want to make your own videos or provide audio content, it may not be as daunting as you might think it is. The video can be as simple as the instructor presenting the same information in the textbook, or a very short clip telling the students what is most important to notice in their textbook. As previously mentioned, it could also be audio only, or audio accompanied by PPT, or illustrations rather than just the teacher's face.

The toughest decision might be deciding which program is the best. Factors to consider include

- Cost: Some are free, others require a one-time purchase, licensing, or other fees.
- Compatibility: Does the program work well with publisher-driven systems that accompany your textbooks or your campus/school course/ learning management system or online platform?
- Content: What exactly do you want to record? Some programs work better with shorter videos; others are better suited to longer, more detailed videos that support other features, such as slides or interactive components.
- Comfort level: How comfortable are you with technology? Some are easier to use than others.

Some programs that have proven successful and popular depending on the instructor and the factors are listed here:

Audacity: www.audacity.sourceforge.net
CamStudio: www.camstudio.org
Camtasia: www.techsmith.com/camtasia.html
Educreations: www.educreations.com/register/
Jing: www.techsmith.com/jing.html
Panopto: www.panopto.com
Screencast: www.screencast.com
Screencast-o-matic: http://www.screencast-o-matic.com/
VoiceThread: www.voicethread.com
YouTube: www.youtube.com

Many schools and universities have course management systems that work well for flipped classrooms. Some are open source, such as Canvas, Moodle, and Sakai. Others are proprietary; therefore, they are protected by some sort of patent, copyright, or trademark. These might not be as useful if you are constrained by a school-owned or school-licensed system. Some popular systems are Blackboard, Edmodo, and GlobalScholar. There are also some systems that might be worth exploring for individual use or classes, such as Tegrity (www.tegrity.com) or StudyMate (http://www.respondus.com/products/studymate/index.shtml).

One other thing to consider in using technology: Consider adopting textbooks that are accompanied by online exercises or websites that feature activities written by professionals that align with the vocabulary and grammar level of the textbook. Some of these systems also do the grading for the instructor, include many comprehension-level activities (making them ideal for students to use on their own), and maintain statistics (such as how often students log in and what their scores are). These programs can be also be used during class time in a school's lab, or after school for students that might not have technology at home.

Lesson Learned

Videos are not required to flip the classroom. However, when videos are used from other sources, it's important to evaluate them just as we do our textbooks. Instructors need to make sure that the content is on target with their course objectives. It can be time-consuming to evaluate video content, but that might be time well spent if you find the right videos. Finding great videos makes it easy to flip the classroom. Additionally, if you want to create your own videos, some programs make it easy and do not require that you be technically savvy. A brief exploration into the variety of programs will help you determine which is best for you and your students. Flipping the classroom does likely mean that the videos will be watched outside of class, so class time can be filled with interactive activities that allow students to demonstrate their knowledge of the content.

4. What About Class Time? (Myth 1: Teachers must create new material for class. Myth 2: An interactive class is already a flipped class.)

A flipped classroom differs from other pedagogical models because it gives teachers the same amount of instructional time. This issue was one of my biggest questions about flipping: If I moved everything (or most everything) I had been doing in class, such as presenting material and ensuring comprehension via practices and exercises, to out of class for students to do on their own, what would I be doing in class? Was I going to have to spend hours of time creating new lessons?

At first glance, flipping "seems" to suggest that an instructor simply moves what was assigned as homework into class instruction and moves what was done in class to homework. But I knew that whatever I moved into class also needed to incorporate tasks higher on Bloom's taxonomy.

One of the other things I had heard from people who flipped was that their classes were now more interactive—i.e., less teacher-centered. So now I knew that I also needed to make sure that the activities assigned in class that used higher-order skills also allowed for student interaction with me as the "guide on the side."

ESL classes are very often interactive. When instructors hear that a class with group work, discussion, and interactive activities are part of a flipped class, a common response is "I already do that, so my classroom must be flipped." This is not necessarily true. Using a speaking or conversation class as an example: Students are in pairs or groups and they're talking; they are reading role-plays, they are discussing questions, and they are TALKING! In grammar or vocabulary classes, students often work in pairs to check answers or read examples of the grammar point in dialogues. While these examples are interactive, they are not interactive in the sense that they do not necessarily require students to move beyond the two lowest levels of Bloom's taxonomy. Reading role-plays or dialogues that are provided proves nothing more than the students see and notice the language taught. They don't actually apply the language, and they certainly aren't analyzing or evaluating.

To illustrate, when teaching words and phrases commonly associated with expressing an opinion, the lesson might present such phrases as "I think," "I believe," "I suppose," "In my opinion," "From my perspective," or "My idea is that." Then a sample dialogue might be presented:

Juan Carlos: Where should we go for lunch?
Jun: Well, I think we should go to the cafeteria in the dorm.
Juan Carlos: We go there all the time. My idea is that we'd go somewhere off campus. I think we should try the new sushi place downtown. Don't you want to go somewhere else?
Jun: Not really. In my opinion, the cafeteria is fast, easy, and close. And I need to stay on campus so I can get to my next class on time.
Juan Carlos: I see what you're saying. I suppose we could go off campus this weekend instead.
Jun: That sounds great.

The dialogue would then be followed by a list of questions for individual work (and then pair work) or discussion, and might require students to underline the opinion language. It might ask them to repeat the dialogue or record it. It might even ask them to write or restate the opinions that the speakers had expressed. The result could be students working together; it may also involve technology if students post their recordings or listen to the passage rather than reading it in print. However, all the action verbs or skills that students need—*read, record, repeat, state, identify, restate, clarify*, etc.—are all Knowledge (Remembering) and Comprehension (Understanding) skills. Even if students are talking and using technology, they are not in a flipped setting. Review the list of action verbs in the section on textbooks for a list of common key verbs for those two lowest levels of Bloom's taxonomy.

Activities and practices that are done in the classroom need to involve actions and thinking that are higher on Bloom's taxonomy. A list of actions/verbs commonly associated with the other levels is provided. Activities or exercises that require use of these skills should be the ones used to fill class time because they are more challenging, require students to use the content from class, and can lead to more success for students (because they are done in the classroom where the instructor becomes the "guide on the side" rather than the "sage on the stage"). Rather than sending students home to work on these types of activities on their own, they can work, even individually, inside the classroom to accomplish these tasks.

Note: Some verbs/actions may fit into more than one category.

List of Verbs Associated With Applying (Now Done Inside the Flipped Classroom)

adapt
apply
complete
demonstrate
develop
dramatize
employ
extend
extrapolate
generalize
infer
interpret
modify
predict
relate
use/utilize

List of Verbs Associated With Analyzing (Now Done Inside the Flipped Classroom)

analyze
appraise
categorize
compare
contrast
criticize
debate
deduce
defend
diagram
discriminate
distinguish
inspect
reason
survey
verify

List of Verbs Associated With Evaluating (Now Done Inside the Flipped Classroom)

- arrange
- argue
- assess
- conclude
- criticize
- decide
- deduct
- defend
- determine
- disprove
- evaluate
- prepare
- prioritize
- rank
- synthesize

List of Verbs Associated With Creating (Now Done Inside the Flipped Classroom)

- anticipate
- build
- collaborate
- compile
- compose
- create
- formulate
- imagine
- integrate
- plan
- propose
- rate
- recommend
- suppose
- test
- theorize

It turns out that filling the class time I now had available was easier than I thought. It was simply a matter of making sure I included activities in which students actually use the content, thus not only improving their English, but also better preparing them for university and professional settings where they actually will have to apply the concepts and not simply memorize facts and figures so they can pass a test.

To give an example, a listening passage in one of the textbooks I use for my listening class is a lecture excerpt about a business topic—marketing. The lecture discusses the four parts of the marketing mix that all begin with the letter P: product, price, place, and promotion. The lecture also touches on covert advertising. The book provides two exercises—one for main ideas and one for details. I used to play the audio in class (sometimes twice if students didn't understand the first time) and confirm comprehension using the main idea and details in practice activities. This more traditional teaching model worked fine, but it had some drawbacks. First, it was much harder to manage class time. I never knew how many times I would have to play the audio to make sure everyone understood. Second, I knew that I was not preparing my students for the college-level work they would eventually need to do because of timing issues. I didn't necessarily have enough class time to put students into groups for an in-depth discussion that would force them to actually apply the concepts they heard about in the lecture, which is exactly what they have to do in any flipped classroom, in most of their mainstream classes, and eventually in a career or job. The textbook has a discussion activity that puts students into "marketing teams," where they create their own electronic game. The questions require them to use the four Ps of the marketing mix. Sometimes I didn't have time to do this at all, thus never exposing my students to the higher-level skills that they will need later. I could ask students to work with their groups outside of class, but then I abandon the "guide on the side" idea and force students to what would be considered higher-level skills on their own.

Flipping solves this problem for me. I assign both the listening and the two exercises as the "homework" now. I don't have to worry about students understanding the lecture because they can listen as many times as they need to; it can be different for everyone and that doesn't affect my class time. Everyone understands the content when they get to class. I also don't have to worry about my class time management. I have enough time to use the discussion activity. Most important, I don't have to worry about filling class time or finding an activity. The discussion activity *is in the textbook* and carefully designed to employ the content from the lecture excerpt.

For example, the textbook I use in my listening class has a page of synthesizing projects and presentations. In the past, I didn't have much time to include these projects as part of my course. Or, if I did, they were assigned as homework and could be challenging for students to complete on their own. To accompany the lecture on the marketing mix, the textbook suggests a project where students choose an advertisement from a magazine or a commercial from television. They then analyze it for the four Ps and offer opinions about what they would do similarly and what they would do differently. Students, for the most part, enjoyed the project, but often needed help when they actually had to apply the four Ps on their own, since the project had been assigned as homework. Now that I had the class time in the flipped setting, we worked on the project in class, and I was there to help students with the actual application of the concepts. What resulted was higher-quality projects, and students reporting that they enjoyed the projects much more when they could work in class with the "guide on the side" and their peers. The caliber of work definitely improved.

The myth that an instructor might struggle to fill class time if they flipped the classroom can also be dispelled with the help of ancillary materials that accompany their chosen textbook. In studying a selection of instructor's manuals, many offer supplemental ideas for discussions and projects. Usually, these extra ideas are perfect for a flipped setting because they would traditionally have been assigned as homework and usually require the higher-level Bloom's taxonomy skills. To continue using the marketing lecture as an example, this idea was provided in the instructor's manual:

> Either broaden the in-depth discussion or ask students to use a product they are familiar with or are interested in to complete this activity. One goal is to help them make connections and synthesize information. Students can use outside sources to do light research. Require them to write a marketing presentation (examples: a competitive analysis or a price analysis that will allow them to talk about the history of the product and its price increases). As part of their report, they should offer advice as to what the company can do to improve the marketing of the product. Remind students to incorporate the language from this unit (comparing/contrasting, advice, and continuation signals). Schedule time for formal presentations if desired and encourage use of PowerPoint or other visual aids. Rubrics can be borrowed or adapted from or created at www.rcampus.com/indexrubric.cfm.

Lesson Learned

Filling class time with a quantity of quality materials is not often a problem. Teachers who flip can make better use of textbook content. There is no need to create brand-new materials. Textbooks are often carefully designed to include all of the skills on Bloom's taxonomy and include variety of activities. Students are also happier when instructors use more of the book that they required students to buy. Even if an instructor doesn't use a textbook, using educational websites and blogs, teacher resource books, or presentations from teaching workshops and conferences provide a wealth of activities and lessons that succeed in a flipped setting.

5. Do I Have To Do It That Way? (Myth: There is only one way to flip.)

In one of my first classroom experiences as an ESL teacher, a student asked the question: what was the best way to proceed with an assignment? All these years later, I don't remember the specific assignment he was asking about, but there was more than one way to approach the project. I answered with an idiom: *There is more than one way to cook an egg*, which is a phrase my mom had used occasionally when I was growing up and it stuck with me. I was reminded of this idiom yet again when I began flipping and faced another question. Is there only one way to flip? No, there is more than one way to cook an egg and there is more than one way to flip a classroom.

It is important to note that ESL teachers do not need to do things exactly as those in other departments or fields are doing them. As discussed, ESL instructors are not likely to provide the same type of 45-, 60-, or 75-minute lectures, and video and technology are not required to flip the classroom. A reading class can use all printed material for both the skills presentation and the practice, and still be flipped.

What other options are there beyond what some people call the "true flip" with lectures on video? Can the flipped model be modified in some way but still be a flipped—as opposed to one of the other models (online or blended learning course)?

The In-Class Flip

The in-class flip is a great option for ESL teachers or settings where there is concern that the "homework" or direct instruction that is supposed to take place outside of class will not actually happen. The reasons could range from not having the hardware (i.e., a computer at home), reliable internet service, time constraints of students, or, sadly, laziness.

In an in-class flip, instructors present the content in class, often using "stations" that are set up around the classroom. This content is often presented in video format at one of the "stations" in the classroom or computer lab. Students watch the video in class and then move through other "stations" to complete activities. The activities can be independent or done as group work, and they are related to the video and/or to other course content. The instructor's role mirrors that of a "true" flipped classroom—moving from student to student or group to group to answer questions and "guide" students with the work.

There are some advantages to the in-class flip. The concern that students do not actually do the homework is minimized. The instructor can see the student watching the video and/or doing the homework. Instructors can keep students focused if they see minds wandering, just as they would do if lecturing as "sage on the stage." Videos can also embed multiple-choice questions to keep students involved, or students can be asked to complete a printed quiz at a station before moving on to other stations. This allows a kind of monitoring, and instructors are there to answer questions and allow struggling students to watch the video again. This kind of flipping session means that no one can claim that they don't have the technology required, and if a student misses school, the stations are still there throughout the day, week, or time period dedicated to that content. If a student misses school for an activity or illness, he or she can proceed through the stations to catch up.

Some possible drawbacks exist. Classroom management will be different depending on class hours and the number of stations. Activities may or may not fit into one class period. The actual classroom might make a difference. Do you need chairs arranged a certain way, do you want to determine which students work together, or are there enough activities planned? (You may want to plan more activities in case some students move through the stations more quickly than others.) Instructors don't always get the same "time back" that would be gained with a "true" flipped classroom because some of the Comprehension/Understanding work is done during class time.

In this model, generally, stations are left "up" for extended periods of time, which has advantages in that students who have been absent can easily come in early or stay late to work their way through the stations and the content remains accessible if students want to watch/practice more than once. The disadvantage is that depending on the activities, you can't move chairs, desks, or tables as readily as you may like.

Partial Flipping

It is not necessary to flip an entire course. Instructors do not have to flip every lesson of every session of the entire course. Flipping can be implemented incrementally. It's not always possible or easy to simply flip an entire course the next time you are scheduled to teach. Options for partial flipping include:

- flip only certain lessons
- flip only parts of lessons
- flip only once or twice a week (or month or quarter or semester)
- flip only certain classes
- flip instructions or procedure directions
- flip certain chapters
- flip final, capstone, or cumulative projects

Flipping Mastery

Mastery learning is an instructional method which was first proposed by Bloom. In this method, students must master a certain level of understanding, usually on some sort of assessment or test, before moving on to the next concept in class. If students do not achieve said mastery, they receive other support and review the material before being assessed (or taking the test) again. When students master the content, they then proceed. While this concept does not always fit well with traditional methods of teaching, it does work well with the flipped model because time required for each student to achieve mastery or understand concepts depends on the students—and in a flipped classroom, students have as much time as they need to understand the content and the benefit of differentiated instruction inside the classroom because there they work with teachers and peers.

Flipping mastery is the combination of the flipped learning and mastery learning concepts and has been advocated by Jonathan Bergmann, one of the teachers credited with starting the flipped model in 2004. Since flipped classrooms eliminate the lectures from the classroom, students no longer need to work at the same pace. In a multi-level classroom, lower-level students don't fall behind (and/or have the "guide on the side" to help them keep up), and upper-level students don't get bored while waiting for the other students to catch up.

For example, class might begin with a mastery check and/or a simple question of who needs extra help. Instructors can offer a variety of learning activities for the class to practice and a variety of tests or assessments that students use to demonstrate mastery. In other words, some activities will be designed for the lower-level students, while others will be more challenging for the students who have already advanced or understand the content. An added bonus is that mastery need not be measured on a test. For students who simply don't do well on tests, these other options, combined with the personalized attention and more frequent feedback, can still display mastery. However, simple tests can work just as well, so test banks or instructor-written tests can make a teacher's life easier.

As with most flipped classrooms, a large part of assessment is formative. Instructors give constant feedback as students work on their activities, worksheets, notes (from the video or book), etc. Instructors can ask a few key questions and quickly identify when students understand or when they don't. This formative assessment is also a chance for instructors to students to do more complex work and to help struggling students understand the essential ideas for mastery. The other type of assessment in flipped classrooms and necessary for a successful flip-mastery class is summative assessment. Most classes have a summative assessment, but the difference is that students can retake a test as often as needed. Instructors can set up appointments or meet with students to discuss the results.

One possible challenge of this model might be that students could move through all the levels more quickly. Instructors might need to plan extra units for students who move faster than others. Also, more summative assessments might be necessary so that faster students don't tell the other students what is on the test if they take it sooner. The obvious advantage is that grades are better. Students who would normally settle for a mediocre grade can't do that anymore and those who are forced to settle for that mediocre grade now have plenty of chances to earn a higher grade.

Explore→Flip→Apply

The Explore→Flip→Apply method has three phases.

1. Explore: Rather than beginning with the direct instruction via a video (or method of choice), teaching begins with a problem or question that students must try to answer. How they find the answer can vary. Instructors/professors in the sciences might be able to assign lab work or some other type of research. However, for ESL, it can be reading or a video. The key is that the students need to learn the basic knowledge and start to learn the content without any instruction from the instructor.

2. Flip: The second phase is the traditional flip (or whatever method has been selected to deliver the direct instruction—a video or reading). The direct instruction includes all the information students need to fully understand the concept and it will help students fill any gaps left from their initial work on solving the presented problem in the Explore phase.
3. Apply: In this final phase, students participate as they would in a flipped classroom. They apply or use some other type of higher-level Bloom's taxonomy skill. Assessment, individualized instruction/ questions, group work, and so on that mirror the traditional flipped classroom is the same.

Peer Instruction

The idea behind peer instruction is similar to flipped learning in that students learn content outside of the classroom and then use that knowledge inside the classroom, usually applying it to a new or unfamiliar context. Direct instruction again takes place outside of class via the method of choice—video, reading, etc.

In advance of the lesson and in class, students answer questions. In high-tech settings, classes may use clickers or web-based polls to submit their responses. In a low-tech setting, students may hold up answers on index cards or display fingers to show their answer choice. These questions allow the instructor to collect responses and learn what is most challenging for students. These challenges might be the ones that are flipped. Instructors then determine what content students should read or watch outside of class.

The peer instruction actually happens in class. Students are asked a question related to the topic of the content they read or watched. Perhaps this question is given at the end of the instruction, but it could also be given at the beginning of class. Students choose and answer and then join another student or a small group. Each student attempts to convince the group that their answer is the best one. At this time, the instructor provides the correct answer. More discussion about what made an answer right or wrong ensues. Instructors are moving from group to group and get to hear what students are discussing and can answer questions as needed.

Where do the questions come from? They can be written by the instructor, but this is also another opportunity to use material in textbooks, instructor's manuals, and test banks.

Asynchronous Options

One last idea is to provide other asynchronous options besides the direct instruction videos or readings. All course materials used in and out of class can be posted on some sort of course management system. Directions or procedural information, student resources, bibliographies, links to useful websites or lectures, and any other useful content can be posted. Many of these sites also include a wiki that all participants can add to. Students often have files or mailboxes where they can submit questions or homework assignments. Discussion boards can also be included so students can still ask questions if they want to get peer or instructor feedback before the next class. Maintaining asynchronous options in addition to, or even in place of, in-class content can offer some benefits to flipped learning, such as individualized instruction or more frequent feedback that would not be part of a more traditional classroom.

If possible or desired, some of these options can also be synchronous. For example, instructors can hold online office hours via Skype or the course management system, announcing certain times that they will be available online outside of class to answer additional questions for individuals. Instructors can also hold office hours for groups, with students asking questions and/or listening to additional notes the instructor wants to provide based on what was done during the previous class period, or to go over instructions that were posted rather than presented in class. The same is true for discussion boards. Teachers can announce certain times and be available online to answer discussion posts as they are posted, rather than waiting until later. Instructors can give small "presentations" on certain books or resources that might be helpful or interesting to the content being covered in class. Or, it can just be time for students to ask for and get more feedback.

Other Ideas

I wanted to flip sooner rather than later, but for teachers who do not need or want to flip immediately, one idea might be to record yourself presenting the material in class. Capturing your direct instruction on video now might provide you with all the videos you need to flip your future classes. Even if these videos are not used for direct instruction in future flipped classrooms, they can be used for review or practice—whether or not the classroom is ever flipped.

Finally, consider enhancing your existing presentations with video or other outside materials. If students don't understand in class, provide videos or materials they can reference outside of class.

Lesson Learned

My mom was right—there is more than one way to cook an egg. Instructors do not need to flip everything! Consider the students and content. While I did start flipping quickly, I did not flip an entire term's worth of material immediately. Start small—flip a lesson or enhance a current lesson with a video. Easing into flipping and carefully considering what you flip will help you decide which is the best method—for the students and for you.

6. What's In It For Me? Or Why Should I Do This? (Myth: Flipping only benefits the students.)

In that original article I read about professors at my university who were flipping their classes, they were quoted as saying that they liked the concept and the change. They said that they felt rejuvenated teaching classes they had taught for years. This information caught my eye. I teach several courses, and I do teach most of them over and over again. They're never quite the same, of course, because I continually update content and every batch of students is just a little different from the one before. For example, teaching writing is something I do every quarter and for which I use the same methods and same textbooks I had been using for years. Rejuvenation sounded good to me.

I could easily see some of the benefits for students—better grades, easier homework, more "exciting" classes that were not so "boring," stronger content knowledge, more critical thinking, more application and skills useful in life after academia, time to understand (individualized or differentiated instruction), etc. That list by itself was appealing, but let me be the first to say that I selfishly wondered what might be in it for me to take that leap of faith and flip my classroom.

Time Factors

I mentioned earlier that classroom time is better managed in a flipped classroom. I want to reiterate that point. Using my writing class as an example, I would present some sort of grammar point or writing strategy in class and then practice that activity to make sure students understood. If all went well, the students understood after one explanation and they all completed the practice sentences at the same time and answered all correctly. All ESL teachers know this just does not happen, however. I am a firm believer in being prepared, so my lesson plans always included far more than I knew I had time for. I would have extra activities and I always wanted to include projects and discussions incorporating higher-level Bloom's skills. However, what happened is what happens to us all. Students asked questions, which took time, and I needed to answer their questions. In those situations, students who did understand and were ready to proceed were forced to sit and wait. Then, at some point, all the students understand (or claim to) and we begin work on the practice activity. This is when the next challenge arises. Advanced students—or those that understood the content—finish before everyone else. They again get "bored" while they wait. Or, I have to stop the less advanced students before they finish.

This type of classroom time-management issue disappears in a flipped setting. When students learn the content on their own and complete the practice activity, they have as much time as they need and when they get to class, everyone should be on the same page. Not only does the instructor now have time to do the activities he or she always wished to do, all the students understand and participate.

Flipped classrooms also affect time outside of class. First, office hours are likely to be used differently. Before flipping, part of my time devoted to office hours was spent explaining content that I had already presented in class to a student who was struggling with it. With the general comprehension-level content moved out of the classroom, this situation does not happen because students already understand. Many of my office hours were also spent working with students on the homework I assigned. Homework before flipping involved skills that were higher on Bloom's taxonomy and harder for students to do, but when students actually have to apply what they are taught, it is much harder to do it when they are home and working alone. After flipping, however, students work on these projects in-class, so the instructor is there to answer questions and provide feedback immediately. Thus, students don't need to visit my office hours for help.

This isn't to say that students don't visit my office hours. They do. However, I did get a lot of time back. I can create activities for my class, work on lesson plans, or grade papers while I'm in my office rather than having to do this in the evenings when I'm at home. Despite the idea that flipping takes a tremendous amount of time at the start, especially if one decides to create their own videos, the time gained back at the end is worth it.

Grading is a fundamental part of an instructor's job and cannot be eliminated; however, flipping does reduce grading time. This reduction can be attributed to several factors. First, with the "harder" work being done in class, the quality of work is better. I no longer have to wonder if they understood me in class; I can see for myself that they did in the quality of work that is produced. As the instructor circulates and helps groups or individuals, questions are answered, suggestions are made, etc., resulting in better work. To continue with my writing class example, we do most of the writing in class. As students work, I move from student to student, making corrections, explaining why changes are needed, and answering questions. Therefore, when I receive, for example, an essay by one of my students, I don't have to edit or correct as much because we worked on it together in class. This drastically reduces grading time.

Students also stop repeating errors. In thinking about a writing class, instructors often collect drafts and then, rightly so, need time to grade those. While taking the time to grade those, classes still move forward. Students will be working on the next assignment before they get any feedback on the previous assignment. The second assignment will be riddled with the same errors as the first. In a flipped setting where formative assessment can be provided more frequently, students can make changes more immediately and those then not only don't appear in the first assignment, but they also disappear in the next assignment.

The benefits of flipped learning on class time, office hour time, and as a result, personal time makes flipping worth it.

Transferability

One of the biggest challenges ESL teachers face is helping students to realize how useful or important English class is. In my EAP (English for Academic Purpose) setting, my students would rather not be in English class. They want to be in mainstream classes in their major fields. My graduate students especially want to be working in their labs or doing research and, even though they know they need the English class and that the class is useful, they don't always perceive it as anything other than "just English class." Many students come to class because they have to. They're not bad students. They do what they're told and they pass the class. Flipping the classroom takes on that issue because the structure allows for use of different skills (necessary for academic and professional success) and greater transferability outside the ESL classroom.

ESL students will often say they learned the skills taught in their ESL textbooks. For example, students know how to skim, scan, and annotate a reading because their ESL teacher taught them how to do it in their reading class. We ESL teachers know they know how to do it because we watched them do it in class. Students do *not* skim, scan, or annotate a reading in their engineering, history, or any other course textbook. Why? I am not sure any of us know the answer to that. I am not sure there is just one answer. Perhaps students just view English class as its own entity. Maybe they can apply these skills to the simple readings we practice with in class. Or, maybe they're just afraid to try this in "real life" because their other classes are "more important" and they can't worry that skimming an engineering chapter might lead them to fail a test.

I sometimes worry that this might also mean that I did not adequately teach the skills. In a traditional reading class, an instructor might teach skimming and scanning skills, practice with the practice exercise in the book, and then send students home with the longer reading in the book with the instructions to skim and scan it. Do students really skim and scan when they are home? Or do they continue to look up words they don't know and read every word? We're not there to check, so we cannot confirm what the student is doing when they are not with us. (And maybe they don't read it at all.) Therefore, flipping a reading class can be a little counter-intuitive. I previously thought that by moving all of the actual reading out of the classroom, I was flipping. However, when we were in class, my students were not necessarily using any of the higher skills; they weren't applying the skimming skills that I had taught them. Moving the reading into the classroom allowed me to help students apply the skills. By flipping, the skill lesson and short practice is done as homework and reading can be moved into the classroom. This model with a reading class gives instructors more class time, which allows time to use more authentic materials. One assignment that has worked very well for me is to ask students to bring in a textbook from one of their other classes. This textbook is what we use in class to practice their reading skills. Allowing students to practice on content they need or want not only makes the English skills transferable, achieving my goal, but also makes my class "more useful" in the eyes of the students. Students get to kill two birds with one stone: complete English class as well as complete reading for another class. If students aren't yet matriculated, this idea is still easily implementable. They can choose a textbook from a field they are interested in, or from an introductory course they are likely to study as part of general education requirements (history, psychology, and so on). The material also need not be a textbook; the skill can be practiced on any reading material—magazines or memos or letters from work or school. Letting students choose any material they care about makes all the difference.

The Humanized Classroom

Salman Khan, the CEO and founder of Khan Academy, has spoken about the humanized classroom. How one defines the word *humanized* might differ, but most instructors who flip claim that their classrooms are more "humanized" than they were before—that they know their students much better than they did before.

In my own experience, I often remember needing several days to memorize names and to match them to faces in my classroom, which could sometimes make taking attendance a challenge during the first few days of class. I also remember times when I would put students into groups. I would call out the names and ask them to sit together, but they couldn't do it because even though I knew all their names, they still didn't know each other's names. I also remember that in the few minutes before class time, students would come in, sit, and then pass the time by opening their books or computers and reading. More likely now, they open their phones and check their social media sites or email. They didn't do much more than greet me or their peers, if that. During class, students did not always ask questions after I presented material. Even if they didn't understand, they wouldn't want to ask a question for fear of holding up the class, especially if they felt the question applied only to them. Even with pair work and group work, which went fine, the classroom was not as student-centered or interactive as it could have been.

A flipped classroom can be a drastically different environment. Flipped instructors get to know their students much better, and students often find the instructor is much more approachable. When students are working on the projects, they may be in groups and they get to know each other much better. Because students are in smaller groups, they are more likely to ask each other or the instructor for help. When students work individually, they ask more individual questions, which is helpful to the instructor because the whole class is not stopped in order to answer a question not everyone has, and helpful to the student because they get to ask their question without holding up the class. Instructors are also less likely to run out of time and will be able to answer all the questions instead of just a few questions.

Because the dynamic of class and groups changes, students get to know each other much better. I have noticed in my classes that when students arrive a few minutes early, they now talk to each other and greet each other by name. When I assign groups and announce names, there is no uncertainty as to who everyone is. They immediately form groups. Additionally, I know students and their needs better from the individual feedback I am able to provide.

This makes me more approachable and less "scary" than the professor who walks into a room, lectures, and then leaves immediately after class. Students are less afraid to ask questions and appreciate the consultant role that instructors play in the flipped classroom. They actually see it as more beneficial rather than less, in part because the classroom is a community and a team—not a government or bureaucracy. All parties benefit.

Lesson Learned

In some ways, the benefits for students and teachers overlap. Earning better grades in English and in other classes is just as much a benefit for students as it is for the instructor. If students get better grades in classes, they often attribute it to English instructors, which could even affect course evaluations. The same is true with students being more engaged, using authentic materials, applying skills to other classes/settings, and so on.

7. In Summary

This e-book addressed some of my questions I initially had about flipped learning. For more details about the advantages of a flipped learning environment, strategies, and textbook samples to use as you begin flipping your classroom, or more resources, please see *Flip It! Strategies for the ESL Classroom*.

In summary, here is what every ESL teacher needs to know before flipping their instruction.

In short, a **flipped learning environment** means:

1. Students study the topic on their own; how that instruction is delivered may or may not be based on technology.
2. Students use classroom time to apply the knowledge they learned.
3. The application can be performed through a variety of activity types (completing exercises, solving problems, analyzing authentic materials, developing group projects, participating in discussions or debates, and the like).
4. The skills listed on Bloom's taxonomy are flipped so that higher-order skills are done in the classroom, not as homework.
5. The instructor is not the "sage on the stage" but a "guide on the side," who mentors or helps students as needed rather than delivering instruction.
6. Students still have homework; it may be more, it may also be less, but it is likely easier than before.
7. Flipped classrooms are not unstructured, uncontrolled environments; the instructor is still a vital part of the learning experience.
8. Flipped classrooms do not replace the teacher. Even if the instructor uses video, students do not spend the bulk of their time at the computer working in isolation as they would in a MOOC or as part of an online course. Rather, the teacher's role is different, leading to a more humanized and consultative relationship with the student. It can be argued that the teacher is actually works even more closely with students and is more approachable than in the traditional model.

9. Flipped learning makes the instructor more valuable because he or she is accessible when the students are working interactively and engaged in learning.
10. Face-to-face time is likely to be more valuable since it will often involve individual, customized feedback. Feedback and assessment is both formative and summative and much more frequent than in a traditional classroom setting.

As far as my own teaching was concerned, I wanted to better serve my students and flipped learning offered me that opportunity. I wanted to make better use of my textbooks, think carefully about what was done inside the classroom and what was done as homework, and liven up my class by doing more than just presenting information, reviewing answers, and giving tests or evaluative assignments.

ESL students often follow instruction and do what they're asked, but could we better prepare them for academic classes? Even more important, could we better prepare them for life beyond academia? Life itself is not a series of multiple choice tests. Students will become employees where they will have to apply skills to their jobs and will have to talk to their supervisors and colleagues about problems, tasks, and other job-related topics. A flipped ESL class can help because it can prepare students to use what we teach and demonstrate their understanding. Since the day I first read about flipped classrooms and flipped my own classes, I honestly have not looked back.

SOURCES CONSULTED AND ADDITIONAL RESOURCES

Bauer-Ramazani, C., Graney, J. M., Marshall, H. W., & Sabieh, C. (2016). Flipped learning in TESOL: Definitions, approaches, and implementation. *TESOL Journal*, 7(2), 429–437.

Bergmann, J., and Sams, A. (2012). *Flip your classroom: Reach every student in every class every day*. Washington, DC: International Society for Technology and Education.

Bloom, B. S. (Ed.) (1956–). *Taxonomy of educational objectives; the classification of educational goals*. New York: Longmans, Green.

Bergmann, J., Overmyer, J., & Wilie, B. (2013). The flipped class: Myths vs. reality. *The Daily Riff*. www.thedailyriff.com/articles/the-flipped-class-conversation-689.php

Classroom Window (2012). Flipped classrooms: Improved test scores and teacher satisfaction. Retrieved from http://classroomwindow.com/flipped-classrooms-improved-test-scores-and-teacher-satisfaction

Ferenstein, G. (2013, September). The flipped classroom boosts grades 5%. Why that's as big as we can expect. *Tech Crunch*. Retrieved from http://techcrunch.com/2013/09/18/the-flipped-classroom-boosts-grades-5-whythats-as-big-as-we-can-expect/

Flipped Learning Network (2014). Available at https://flippedlearning.org

Gerstein, J. (n.d). The flipped classroom. Resources compiled at www.scoop.it/tlthe-flipped-classroom

Gifford, D. (2013, January 10). Flipped classroom gaining popularity among profs. The Stanford Daily.

Hoag, C. (2013, January 27). Teachers flip for "Flipped Learning" class model. Available at http://bigstory.ap.org/article/teachers-flip-flipped-learning-class-model

Khan, S. (2012). *The one world schoolhouse: Education reimagined*. New York: Hachette Book Group.

Kostka, I., & Brinks Lockwood, R. (2015). What's on the internet for flipping English language instruction? *The Electronic Journal for English as a Second Language*, 19(2), 1–12.

Learn Spark (n.d.). Flipped classroom. Available at http://learn-spark.blogspot.com/2012/09/Aipped-classroom.html

Lockwood, R. B. (2014). *Flip it! Strategies for the ESL classroom.* Ann Arbor: University of Michigan Press.

Lytle, A. D. (2013). Flipping the classroom. *HEIS News: The Newsletter of the Higher Education Interest Section.* Alexandria, VA: TESOL.

Marshall, H. (2013). Three reasons to flip your classroom. *Bilingual Basics: The Newsletter of the Bilingual Interest Section and Teachers of English to Deaf Students.* Alexandria, VA: TESOL.

Mehring, J. G. (2016). Present research on the flipped classroom and potential tools for the ESL classroom. *Computers in the Schools*, 33(1), 1–10.

Mehring, J. G., & Leis, A. (Eds.). (2017). *Innovations in flipping the language classroom: Theories and practice.* New York: Springer.

Meyer, R. (2013, September 13). The post-lecture classroom: How will students fare? The Atlantic. http://www.theatlantic.com/technology/archive/2013/09/the-post-lecture-classroom-how-wilI-students-fare/279663

Overmyer, J. (2013). The flipped learning network. https//flippedlearning.org

Ray-Trevino, S. (2013). Changing the focus to 21st century skills: One educator's experience. *The Language Educator*, 8(3), 22–23.

Webb, M., & Doman, E. (2016). Does the flipped classroom lead to increased gains on learning outcomes in ESL/EFL contexts? *The CATESOL Journal*, 28(1), 39–59.

Wills, C. (2012). Flipped classroom. Retrieved from http://learn-spark.blogspot.com/2012/09/flipped-classroom.html